INCLUDING SHOOTER

A DRAMA BY
Nicholas C. Pappas

The Rules in Brief

1) Do NOT perform this Play without obtaining prior permission from Playscripts, and without paying the required royalty.

2) Do NOT photocopy, scan, or otherwise duplicate any part of this book.

3) Do NOT alter the text of the Play, change a character's gender, delete any dialogue, cut any music, or alter any objectionable language, unless explicitly authorized by Playscripts.

4) DO provide the required credit to the author(s) and the required attribution to Playscripts in all programs and promotional literature associated with any performance of this Play.

For more details on these and other rules, see the opposite page.

Copyright Basics

This Play is protected by United States and international copyright law. These laws ensure that authors are rewarded for creating new and vital dramatic work, and protect them against theft and abuse of their work.

A play is a piece of property, fully owned by the author, just like a house or car. You must obtain permission to use this property, and must pay a royalty fee for the privilege—whether or not you charge an admission fee. Playscripts collects these required payments on behalf of the author.

Anyone who violates an author's copyright is liable as a copyright infringer under United States and international law. Playscripts and the author are entitled to institute legal action for any such infringement, which can subject the infringer to actual damages, statutory damages, and attorneys' fees. A court may impose statutory damages of up to $150,000 for willful copyright infringements. U.S. copyright law also provides for possible criminal sanctions. Visit the website of the U.S. Copyright Office (www.copyright.gov) for more information.

THE BOTTOM LINE: If you break copyright law, you are robbing a playwright and opening yourself to expensive legal action. Follow the rules, and when in doubt, ask us.

Playscripts, Inc.
7 Penn Plaza, Suite 904
New York, NY 10001

toll-free phone: 1-866-NEW-PLAY
email: info@playscripts.com
website: www.playscripts.com

This play is for the incredible AW.
Without her, it wouldn't exist.
Honey, I owe it all to you.

Cast of Characters

The Shooter

JAMES (also the CAMERAMAN, BARTENDER, COACH, HECKLER, SPONSOR, MODERATOR, and STEVE)

Students

ROBERT

MIKE

RALEIGH

SEAN

MEGAN

JANELLE

MOLLY

SARA

The Killers

WHITMAN (also BULKY MAN)

LANZA (also DAVID)

CHO (also REPORTER)

HARRIS (also GROUP LEADER)

KLEBOLD (also SOUND GUY)

RODGER (also EDDIE)

SPENCER (also YOUNG LADY)

Act 1 Voices (Pre-recorded)

MOM, FATHER, BULLY, KC, MARCELLE, SARAH WITH AN *H*, DOUGHNUT GUY, DAD

Production Notes

Set

The set is flowing. In act 2, I described several of the locations in some detail. I did that for mood more than actual set. The play can be done with wooden blocks, stage blacks, and a strong lighting design.

Sound

I feel like this play lives and dies by its sound design. In act 1, those noises should almost feel as if they are coming from within our own heads. They should be all encompassing and impossible to blot out. In act 3, I'm hoping the soundscape sets the mood and tone of each location.

Tone

Yes, this play is about a very serious subject. I think the words and what the audience brings to the play will be heavy enough. I think, at times, it's important to look for the levity. Remember, these people lived through it. To them, as awful as it is, it's simply life. Janelle should be the first person to cry. Let the others help build the audience to this cathartic release.

Pace

Speed is key in act 1. Act 2 can take its time. Act 3 is a roller coaster.

Acknowledgments

First reading direction by Carolyn Cork Greer, dramaturgy by Dominic Orlando.

All production groups performing this play are required to include the following on the title page of every program:

2014 *Dramatics* Magazine commission play

INCLUDING SHOOTER
by Nicholas C. Pappas

ACT 1

(BEEP! BEEP! BEEP!
A screaming alarm clock is the only thing visible. The beeping grows louder and louder until it's unbearable.
WHAP!
Nine hands, seemingly from nowhere, come slapping down on it at once.
The alarm clock disappears along with its sound. Silence.
Darkness a moment.
Was that a dream?
Out of the ether, nine teenagers appear. They stand in a line facing front. Unmoving. Like statues.
On the far end is a boy named JAMES.
After a moment, JAMES's head turns. Only his head. He looks at the other kids for a long time before he faces front again, falling into line. He tries his hardest to fit in.
Soon, JAMES gets an itch on his nose. It drives him crazy. At first he does that thing where he wiggles his nose and contorts his face. It does little to help.
He just can't stand it anymore!!
He has to scratch.
He does.
Sweet, sweet relief.
He breaks ranks and walks down the line of teens, taking the time to look each one up and down.
He even tries to stand and pose like some of them…with no luck. He's just too different.
After some deliberation, he steps up behind ROBERT. Touches him on the shoulder. The touch is a single finger tap that suggests "excuse me, I don't mean to disturb you."
The second the touch lands—
BAM BAM BAM BAM BAM.
A hard rapping on an invisible door. ROBERT is quickly getting ready for school. He's frantic. JAMES follows ROBERT's motions, like a shadow.)

ROBERT. Almost ready, Mom.

MOM. *(Offstage:)* Hurry up.

ROBERT. I'm trying.

MOM. *(Offstage:)* If you're late to school, you'll miss out. And then you'll be an idiot. Don't be an idiot.

> *(This gives both ROBERT and JAMES pause.)*

ROBERT and JAMES. I'm not an idiot.

> (ROBERT *quickly finishes getting ready.* JAMES *has stopped the shadowing. Like that,* ROBERT *is gone, off to school.*
> JAMES *looks at the line of students and settles his gaze on* RALEIGH. *Like he did with* ROBERT, JAMES *steps up behind* RALEIGH *in a "shadow spot." A heavy, intrusive tap on the shoulder—*
> WHIRRRR!!!!
> *A loud whistle blows.* RALEIGH/JAMES *are down on the ground doing push-ups. Fast. Hardcore.)*

FATHER. *(Offstage:)* Faster. Faster!!

> *(The boys work faster.)*

FATHER. *(Offstage:)* You don't want to be weak. Are you weak?

RALEIGH and JAMES. I'm not weak!

RALEIGH. —Sir!

FATHER. *(Offstage:)* Go get me some laps!

> (RALEIGH *is up on his feet and running, sprinting off the stage.* JAMES *watches him go from his position on the ground. He lays there a moment out of breath, arms sore.*
> *After a moment he collects himself, is up on his feet.*
> *He looks at the students and walks toward* MEGAN. *He reaches out to tap her, but decides against it. Goes to tap* MIKE, *but again, something stops him.*
> *He quietly does the "Eeny, meeny, miny, moe" thing. It still doesn't help him decide.*
> *An idea hits him.*
> *He stands between the two and taps them both on the shoulder as if he is trying to jump into the conversation.*
> THUMP! THUMP! THUMP!
> MEGAN *and* MIKE *come alive playing basketball. Their sneakers squeak on the court.* JAMES *takes turns shadowing both of them.)*

MEGAN. I'ma drive the lane—

MIKE. You can't even drive a car.

MEGAN. Watch this!

> *(She steps toward him. He counters by moving back into a defensive position.*

She counters that with a jump shot.
They all watch the ball sail over their heads.
CLANK!
The ball bounces off the rim.)

MIKE. Brick.

BULLY. *(Offstage:)* Nice shot, dyke.

MIKE. Not cool.

MEGAN. Mike.

(MIKE looks in the direction of the bully. A death glare.)

MEGAN. Mike.

(He looks at her.)

MEGAN. Forget it.

BULLY. *(Offstage:)* Yeah. Forget it, faggot! You and your sick-in-the-head friend should get off my court.

(MEGAN lunges after him to take a swing. MIKE holds her back.)

MIKE. He's not worth it.

MEGAN and JAMES. I'm not sick in the head.

MIKE and JAMES. And don't call people faggot.

MIKE. It makes you look like a backwards idiot.

MEGAN. I'll kill him. I swear.

(JAMES looks at her quizzically when she says this.
MIKE has calmed MEGAN down enough to get her to walk away,
which they do. JAMES, alone, mimics a basketball dribble and shot.
He misses.
Another look at the students.
Takes his shadow position behind JANELLE. The kindest shoulder
tap—
DO-DO-DO-DO!!!
The sound of two kids doing the final Jeopardy theme song.)

JANELLE. Uhhhh.

KC. *(Offstage:)* What's the answer?

JANELLE. Give me a sec.

MARCELLE. *(Offstage:)* You're never going to pass if you don't study.

JANELLE. I studied, Marcelle.

KC. *(Offstage:)* It's easy. Are you retarded or something?

JANELLE and JAMES. Don't call me retarded.

KC. *(Offstage:)* I'm just saying.

JANELLE. KC, don't be a bitch.

> *(She turns on her heel and walks away in a huff. Leaving* JAMES *alone again.*
> *He looks like he wants to talk. Even opens his mouth to do so, but can't.*
> *Scans students.*
> *Shadow position.*
> *He goes to tap* MOLLY, *but it's full of love. More of a caress. It's like touching a long-lost but now married lover. He makes contact—* MOLLY *slaps her hands together. A single clap in a "eureka" moment. The chatter of a busy doughnut/coffee shop.)*

MOLLY. I know what I want! A glazed doughnut. But cut it in half, toast it, and put cream cheese on it?

DOUGHNUT GUY. *(Offstage:)* Excuse me?

MOLLY. Glazed doughnut, toasted like a bagel, with cream cheese.

DOUGHNUT GUY. *(Offstage:)* Seriously?

MOLLY. Yeah. Why?

DOUGHNUT GUY. *(Offstage:)* It'll make you fat. You don't want that. You're such a cute little thing.

MOLLY and JAMES. Don't judge people by their appearance.

DOUGHNUT GUY. *(Offstage:)* Don't be fat. Easy fix.

MOLLY. Wow. Just… Wow.

> *(DING-DONG. The door chimes as she walks out of the doughnut shop leaving* JAMES *there, standing in the deepest embarrassment.*
> *He's not as strong as* MOLLY.
> *He wants an escape.*
> *Scan. Finds* SARA. *Shadow position. Hesitant tap.*
> *The chatter of a crowded school hallway.* SARA *sets into motion, trying to avoid someone's gaze.)*

SARAH WITH AN H. *(Offstage:)* Sara? Hey.

> *(SARA looks in the direction she was trying to avoid two seconds earlier.)*

SARAH WITH AN H. *(Offstage:)* Did you get my friend request?

SARA. Just because you're popular doesn't mean you have to mess with me!

SARAH WITH AN *H*. *(Offstage:)* I'm not—

SARA and JAMES. *(Screaming:)* Quit making fun of me!!

> (SARA *looks shocked that she has yelled this. She covers her mouth and runs off.*
> JAMES *remains.*
> *His hurt turns to an extreme anger.*
> *With a certain kind of determination we've not seen before, he approaches the final teen and taps him on the shoulder. It's the tap of an angry best friend.*
> *POP! POP! POP!*
> *Loud video game noises fill the space. It's* Call of Duty, *a first-person shooter set in a war zone.*
> SEAN *is in the middle of a high-intensity multiplayer game of* Call of Duty. *He speaks into a headset.)*

SEAN. I guess I'll just have to make you my bitch!

DAD. *(Offstage:)* Language.

SEAN. Sorry, Dad.

DAD. *(Offstage:)* No sorries. Turn that crap off.

SEAN. Dad.

DAD. *(Offstage:)* Off. Now. Or I'll show you the sting of my belt.

> (SEAN/JAMES *puts the controller down.)*

DAD. *(Offstage:)* Playing that crap will make you a violent deviant.

SEAN and JAMES. I'm not going to turn into a—

SEAN.—violent deviant.

> (SEAN *looks at* JAMES *when he doesn't finish the sentence with him.*
> JAMES *shrugs his shoulders.*
> SEAN *speaks directly to* JAMES.)

SEAN. James—

JAMES. Go.

> *(They look at each other for a second.)*

JAMES. GO!

> (SEAN *goes.*
> JAMES *is alone.*
> *He feels that.*
> *It weighs on him.*
> *He whispers into the darkness:)*

JAMES. Hello?

> *(Nothing.*
> *A bit louder:)*

Hello?

> *(Nothing.*
> *He screams:)*

HELLO?!?

> *(It echoes through the room…but nothing else.*
> *He simply speaks:)*

Can anybody hear me?

> *(A cacophony of sound:*
> *The beating knuckles on the door.*
> *The ear-splitting whistle.*
> *The thumping basketball bouncing and the sneakers squeaking.*
> *Two kids mocking with the Final Jeopardy song.*
> *The din of a busy doughnut shop.*
> *Teens in a crowded school locker hallway. Lockers slamming.*
> *People shouting and squealing.*
> *The realistic gunfire of* Call of Duty.
> JAMES's *head looks like it's going to explode with sound. He covers*
> *his ears. He is near tears. He is shouting, frantically repeating:)*

JAMES. I'm not an idiot. I'm not sick in the head. Don't call people faggot. I'm not weak. Don't call me retarded. Don't judge people by their appearances. Quit making fun of me. I'm not going to turn into— Can anybody hear me? I'm—

> *(He continues screaming the unbroken chain of dialogue, but he is*
> *all cried out of tears.)*

—not an idiot. I'm not sick in the head. Don't call people faggot. I'm not—

> *(The painful wounds turn to calluses.)*

—weak. Don't call me retarded. Don't judge people by their appearances. Quit making fun—

> *(He hardens.)*

—of me. I'm not going to turn into— Can anybody hear me?

> *(The noise stops.*
> *It's dead silent.*
> JAMES *is on his feet.*
> *Almost emotionless, he starts to get ready for his last day on earth.)*

I'm not an idiot.

(As he speaks, he picks up gun after gun…)

I'm not sick in the head.

(…and makes sure they are loaded.)

Don't call people faggot.

(He slides the weapons into a backpack or places it on his person.)

I'm not weak.

(He's going to war.)

Don't call me retarded.

(His speech is calm.)

Don't judge people by their appearances.

(Accepting of fate:)

Quit making fun of me.

(He is finished packing for his day.)

I'm not going to turn into—

(He takes one last look around.)

Hello?

(He takes his environment in.)

Can anybody hear me?

(Nothing.)

I just want to feel better.

(Blackout.
Long silence.
From the far away distance is the POP, POP, POP sound of gunfire.
As it gets closer, the sound of screaming students comes into focus.
People banging on doors to get inside.
The school bell sounds.
POP, POP, POP!!
The sound is right on top of us.
Cries of pain.
The noise morphs into the sound of static from a TV.
All of a sudden…)

ACT 2

Sara—The Set of a Newsmagazine Show

(...It's the Dateline NBC *theme music. A* REPORTER *stands speaking to the "camera.")*

REPORTER. Most of us remember where we were when we first heard the news coverage on the day James Smith walked into Lincoln High School and opened fire—killing fourteen, including himself, and injuring nineteen others. It's been ten years and *Dateline* is back in this sleepy community to talk with several of the students involved and see how surviving has affected their lives.

(The scene opens up to reveal two chairs facing each other. SARA *sits in one. A* SOUND GUY *is putting the finishing touches on* SARA. *She groans.)*

SOUND GUY. You okay?

SARA. I'm totally nervous.

SOUND GUY. You'll be great. Just be yourself.
And speak clearly.

(The REPORTER *takes his seat across from* SARA.)

REPORTER. Ready?

SOUND GUY. She's nervous.

REPORTER. No need to be. It's not live. We're just getting a raw footage interview.

SARA. What's that mean?

REPORTER. I'll ask you a bunch of questions. Get your answers.
Just be yourself.
We'll do it a couple of times, a couple of different ways with different questions. Open up different parts of your mind.
You guide me.
Then, we edit it all in post-production to make one interview.
I promise we won't make you look bad.

(The SOUND GUY *is finished and checks the reporter's mic.)*

SARA. Thank you.

(The REPORTER *smiles. The* SOUND GUY *leaves.
A* CAMERAMAN, *played by* JAMES, *stands behind the* REPORTER, *pointing his camera at* SARA.)*

REPORTER. We rolling?

CAMERAMAN. Yup.

REPORTER. Great.
You ready?

SARA. Yeah.

REPORTER. We'll start easy.
What's your name?

SARA. I'm Sara.
There's no *H* at the end of that when you put it up on the screen.

REPORTER. That seems important to you.

SARA. Yes.
Not really.
Well.
It's kinda part of my identity.

REPORTER. Identity?

SARA. Yeah. In high school I would flip out if I went to Starbucks and the barista put my name on the cup spelled with an *H*.

REPORTER. Why is that?

SARA. Sarah with an *H* was kind of a bitch.
Not really…
I shouldn't say that about her now that she's—
…
You know—
…

REPORTER. Dead?

SARA. Yeah.
…
Dead.

> (*The* REPORTER *consults his notes.*)

REPORTER. You are speaking of Sarah Denvers, yes? Victim eleven?

SARA. Yes. We never really got along after seventh grade.

REPORTER. You got along before that?

SARA. We were totally best friends before that.

REPORTER. What did she do? Or was it you that did something?

SARA. *She* started hanging out with different people.
She got boobs faster than most of the other girls—
Doesn't surprise me, have you seen her mother?—
Anyway— All the boys wanted to talk to her and she started wearing shirts that, let's just say, showed off her assets. I told her it was stupid

and that the only reason boys talked to her was because of fat and flesh, but she totally got pissed and said I was just angry because I belonged to the itty bitty titty committee.

She wasn't lying, but she didn't have to be so rude about it.

Anyway, all those boys hanging around made her popular with the popular girls and I was left standing outside the circle as they laughed and giggled in the hallway like a bunch of idiotic chimps.

REPORTER. Get any revenge?

SARA. What?

REPORTER. Did you seek retribution?

SARA. Well, I knew I still had my books.

And I knew I was going to be better than her someday.

REPORTER. Really?

SARA. Yeah. That was totally going to be my revenge. I'd come back from a big important work trip in Zurich and on my way back to my big fancy apartment in whatever big metropolitan city I was living in at the time, I'd swing by here to visit my parents for a weekend. And my mom would ask me to go to the store and pick up some milk, and I wouldn't even ask for her credit card because I could afford to buy milk for my parents.

And there would be Sarah with an *H* at the McDonalds in the Walmart…because there is nothing worse than working at a fake McDonalds in a Walmart.

And she'd wave me over and tell me about her deadbeat husband and her fourteen brats running around and I'd smile and nod.

I wouldn't even tell her about my success.

I'd let her guess at it.

And when she finally got around to asking me how I was doing, I'd say "well, I can afford two boob jobs, but unlike you I don't need a nice rack to have people pay attention to me."

Then I'd make her ring me up for my milk and I'd hand her my black American Express card and beam.

It sounds so stupid now.

REPORTER. It sounds like the mind of a teen.

SARA. Yeah.

I guess.

Thank you.

> (SARA *wants to say something but hides it. Badly.*)

REPORTER. What is it?

SARA. Nothing.

REPORTER. It'll make you feel better.
Don't you want to feel better?

SARA. Yeah.

REPORTER. Well? Tell us.

SARA. Two weeks before it happened, she sent me a friend request on Facebook—
I've never told anyone this...
I didn't respond.
I thought it was a trick, like she was totally going to be mean to me or something.
After it happened—
You know—
When James—
...
Happened—
I saw that on the night before the shooting she sent me a private message apologizing for everything. She had wanted to make up for a long time but didn't know how to start.
She felt bad.
And—

> *(She fights tears for the first time. She wins the battle.)*

Can we stop this?

REPORTER. No.
What's going on in your head?

SARA. What?

REPORTER. What are you thinking?

SARA. I'm going to look like a horrible person.
Everyone deifies the dead.
I'm just telling you what I thought then. I don't want to—

REPORTER. Just say it.
Everyone understands.
It'll make you feel better.
And we can always cut it later if you want to.

SARA. Really?

> *(He hesitates just a moment too long, but she doesn't catch it.)*

REPORTER. Sure.

SARA. On the day of the shooting, she waved at me in the hallway.
She assumed I saw the message.
I guess.

I—

...

I flipped her off.

Again, thinking it was all a trick or something. If I had only checked my messages before school, I would have waved back...

REPORTER. Did the message offer an explanation for her actions?

SARA. Kinda.

In the private message, she said the reason she hadn't tried anything before was because I had been so cold to her every time she tried to open that door to renewed friendship.

I guess I held a grudge 'cause I thought she hated me... When in reality I hated her.

I guess she didn't think much about me for all those years.

Don't hold grudges. They're emotionally inefficient and they sap your time and energy.

And no good comes of it.

REPORTER. You were kids.

Do you blame either of you for that grudge?

SARA. I mean, she was young and dumb when she walked away. Only 12.

And I know that we were only 17 when it happened, but I guess in those five years she grew up and I kind of remained the child.

And then she was dead.

REPORTER. What's changed for you in all these years?

SARA. I don't want to go to Zurich anymore.

And I don't mind as much when I go to Starbucks and the barista adds an *H* to the end of my name.

(*They are both quiet for a long time.*)

REPORTER. Let's take a little break and do it again.

Maybe cry next time.

(*Black.*)

Robert—A Bar

(*Jukebox plays softly. The clack of billiard balls slamming into each other. Some sports game on the TV.*

ROBERT, *about 22 years old, is belly up to a bar at the kind of establishment that gives you tetanus just by looking at it.*

He is drunk.*

The BARTENDER *[played by* JAMES*] refills his glass with a cheap well whiskey.*
A young lady approaches the bar.)

BARTENDER. What can I get you?

YOUNG LADY. Cranberry juice and vodka.

(ROBERT *looks her up and down. He likes what he sees. She wants nothing to do with* ROBERT.)

ROBERT. Hi.

YOUNG LADY. Hello.

ROBERT. I—I'm Robert.

YOUNG LADY. Hi Robert.

(She turns her back to him.)

ROBERT. Ha— Have you li—lived here all your life?

(She ignores him.)

ROBERT. Um, excu— Excuse me?
Have— Have you lived here your whole life?

YOUNG LADY. No.
I just moved here.

ROBERT. I have.
Lived my whole life here.
You— You know about what happened at Lincoln High School?
Like—like fou— No. Umm... Six! Six years ago?

YOUNG LADY. The shooting thing?

ROBERT. Yeah!

YOUNG LADY. Everybody knows about that.

ROBERT. What you don't know...
I was there.
I was in—in a hall—a hallway.

(She can't tell if he's kidding or not. But he has her attention. And that's exactly what he wants.)

YOUNG LADY. No way.

ROBERT. Yeah.
I almost stopped it.

YOUNG LADY. You what?

ROBERT. Yeah.

(She's listening now.)

ROBERT. Pop. Pop. Pop. It's what the gun sounded like.
It echoed down the hallway.
Firecrackers?
Nobody thought anything of it. Until—
Until we heard the screaming.
You hear about stuff like that. See it on the news or whatever.
I always liked to think I was the kind of person to do something about it. Be, I don't know, like a hero.
Batman or Superman or Iron-guy or something. Like I seriously planned this out.
It's, uhh—pretty awesome.

(The BARTENDER *gives her the drink she ordered.)*

ROBERT. If you need to get back to—

YOUNG LADY. It's okay.

(She leans into him.)

So what was your plan?

ROBERT. Well, hello beautiful. How did I get so lucky?

(He reaches out and caresses her face with his finger. She pulls back slightly.)

ROBERT. Sorry.

YOUNG LADY. Yeah. Just don't—

ROBERT. I won't do it again. It's just… Difficult.

YOUNG LADY. I'm sure.

(She reaches out and touches his arm. He smiles.)

YOUNG LADY. Your plan?

ROBERT. Right.
I thought if I tossed something at the dude, 'cause it's always a dude, like really chucked something at him, like a book or something, I thought it could give me enough time to charge the guy.
Like, 'cause he'd duck.
Because that's what a person does when something flies at his face.
And then I'd run zig-zag patterns or something, so he can't hit me.
And if he did, it'd just be a flesh wound or whatever. And a cool scar.
And I'd tackle him. Knock him to the ground. I could wrestle the gun away. Then pop, pop.
I'd put two in him.
But only his knees.

I wouldn't kill him.

I'd want to.

Want to make him answer for what he did and shit. Maybe get some answers for the families of the kids who didn't make it. Maybe that'd make it easier for them or something. 'Cause I always see those families crying on TV or whatever when this kind of thing happens and I always wonder why someone didn't do something.

I mean, it would just take two kids, two brave kids, running from different directions or something. One might get hit. But…

…

…

Plan for this kind of thing. With a friend. Or by yourself.

Think of all the dates I could of had. All the girls would have wanted me.

Right?

> *(Somewhere in the story he stops hitting on the girl and becomes wrapped up in his own memories. Living it again.)*

YOUNG LADY. Sure.

But I thought you said you stopped him.

ROBERT. No.

I said almost.

YOUNG LADY. Oh my God! Did you get shot?

> *(ROBERT laughs.)*

ROBERT. No.

YOUNG LADY. What happened?

ROBERT. The pop-pops were coming closer.

Closer.

Closer.

> *(She leans in just the slightest. Closer to him.)*

ROBERT. And tears.

I couldn't stop crying.

See, I knew when I heard the screaming I wasn't going to do it.

Charge him, I mean.

I'm weak.

And I couldn't stop thinking of my mom and dad.

And what they'd look like on TV.

> *(He drinks his drink. She doesn't exist.)*

YOUNG LADY. That's awful.

ROBERT. Yeah.

Yeah.

...

Yeah.

(*He's crawled into his drink. Wants nothing to do with her. He's reached his oblivion.*
A table in the bar laughs really hard at something someone just said. She walks away.
ROBERT *motions to his drink. The* BARTENDER *refills it for him.*)

BARTENDER. If you keep telling people that shit, I'll kick you out of here.

(ROBERT *nods his head. Fight back? Naw. He's a coward.*)

ROBERT. Fair enough.

(*Black.*)

Megan and Mike—High School Reunion

(*Dance music plays softly. The hushed din of a cocktail party. Someone out there has a distinctive laugh.*
MEGAN *sits at a circular table. She wears a simple rack-bought black dress that almost fits her well. She looks uncomfortable.*
A name tag on her chest says "Hi, I'm Megan."
A man in a suit [his name tag says "David"] approaches with two punch glasses.)

DAVID. What's the other one's name?

MEGAN. What?

DAVID. The tag.
If that one is named Megan, I assume the other boob has a name.

(*She shakes her head.*)

MEGAN. You are such a dork.

(*He smiles.*)

DAVID. You married this dork.

(*He kisses her sweetly. Hands her a glass of punch.*
They sit in silence.)

DAVID. Not sure why your school is having a reunion.

MEGAN. James doesn't need to rob us of everything.

(*He gives her a look. What an amazing woman.*)

DAVID. This is kind of depressing.

MEGAN. "Kind of" is being kind.

> *(They sit in a silence a moment. Two good-looking men [the name tags say "Mike" and "Eddie"] in suits enter and make a beeline for them.)*

MIKE. Oh! My! God!

MEGAN. Mike?!?

MIKE. Megan!!

> *(She's on her feet. They hug.)*

MIKE. You look so good. It's been—

MEGAN. Way too long.

MIKE. Yeah. Yeah.

MEGAN. You look fantastic.

MIKE. Thank you. Do say more.

> *(MEGAN laughs.)*

MEGAN. Oh. Sorry. This is my husband David.

MIKE. This is my husband Eddie.

DAVID. Hello.

EDDIE. Nice to meet you.

MEGAN. Oh my god. I can't believe you're gay.

MIKE. I can't believe you're not.

MEGAN. Wait.
What?
Oh my god!
What a freaking surprise!

MIKE. You're telling me.

> *(To EDDIE:)*

She was a crazy basketball star.
Super sporty.

> *(To MEGAN:)*

I thought for sure you were a dyke.
No offense.

MEGAN. None taken. *(Playfully:)* But that's an awful stereotype, calling all sporty girls dykes. You should know better.

EDDIE. He thinks he can get away with it because he's a modern gay man.
I tell him he can't.

(EDDIE *playfully slaps* MIKE's *arm.*)

MEGAN. I like this one. Keep you on your toes.
And from what I remember playing basketball with you, you need that.

EDDIE. Ouch!

MEGAN. And for the record, I am still sporty.

(*She lifts up her dress to show that she's wearing soft combat boots with no heel [think somewhere in between Doc Martens and biker boots] under the dress. They all laugh.*)

DAVID. Please sit with us. Add some life to this table.

EDDIE. Thank you.

(*The foursome sit.*
MEGAN *keeps looking at* MIKE *with a sly little smile.*)

MIKE. What is it?

MEGAN. Shut up and let me look at you.
I haven't seen that face…
Where did you go?

EDDIE. Journey of self-discovery.

MIKE. And Eddie discovery.

(*Laughs all around.*)

MEGAN. Fu—
I can't believe this.
It explains so much.

DAVID. What?

MEGAN. I wanted you so bad in high school.

(*To* DAVID:)

Sorry honey.

EDDIE. Please take him.

MEGAN. Thanks. But I'm quite happy with this one. Traded up, no offense.

(*She gives* DAVID *a little smooch.*)

MIKE. None taken. He's quite a specimen.

DAVID. That's what I keep telling her.

> *(They all laugh again.)*

MIKE. What have you been up to?

MEGAN. Well… I played college basketball on a scholarship. It's where I met David.
Almost made the WNBA, but it wasn't in the cards. Now I'm a defensive coach at the University.

MIKE. No?

MEGAN. Yup.

MIKE. That's so perfect.
Kids?

> *(DAVID hops in. Perhaps too fast.)*

DAVID. No.

MIKE. Oh?

MEGAN. I can't have kids.
They were hopeful, but I just have too much scar tissue.

EDDIE. From what?

MIKE. Eddie.

MEGAN. *(To MIKE:)* It's okay.

> *(To EDDIE:)*

I was shot at the school.

EDDIE. Sorry.

MEGAN. You didn't do it.
How about you guys?
Kids?

EDDIE. Two.

MIKE. Adopted.

> *(MEGAN starts laughing.)*

MEGAN. No shit!

> *(They all find the humor in it. The laughter dies away. It's a moment of silence. Not quite uncomfortable yet.)*

MEGAN. Oh! Did *Dateline* call you about that anniversary special?

MIKE. Yes. How tacky. Who would actually do that? It's disgusting.

> *(A small moment.)*

MEGAN. I'm doing it.

MIKE. I didn't—
I'm sorry.
I was just—

MEGAN. I'm kidding.

MIKE. Oh god.
You bitch.
God.
I didn't know how I was going to talk myself out of that one.

EDDIE. That's a first.

MIKE. Oh, you stop acting all tough.

> *(Their turn to share a little smooch.*
> *Old friends: the table can't help but smile.*
> *A man wearing a "Steve" name tag [played by JAMES] approaches*
> *the table.)*

STEVE. Hey! Megan. Mike… Dudes I didn't go to school with.

MIKE. Steve?

STEVE. Yup. Look. This place sucks. A bunch of us are gonna get out of here. Hit up the White Horse.

MEGAN. Thanks. We'll catch up with you in a little bit.

STEVE. Yeah?

MIKE. Yeah. Sounds awesome man. Thanks for the invite.

> *(STEVE is gone.)*

DAVID. You want to go?

MEGAN. God no.

MIKE. It's terrible, but it's the only way to get rid of that guy.

MEGAN. Just agree with the plan or you'll hear for an hour why you're wrong.

MIKE. That guy was always disrupting our lives.

EDDIE. Some things never change.

MEGAN. I bet he's the only one going to the White Horse.

DAVID. Oh no. That's terrible!

MIKE. No. That's survival.

> *(A laugh.)*

MEGAN. Man, I forgot that guy even existed.

(For the first time, no one has anything to say.)

MIKE. I can't believe how dead this place is.

MEGAN. Yeah. The last time it was this somber some kid shot the place up.

(MEGAN and MIKE laugh. The other two don't.)

DAVID. Megan—

MIKE. You're terrible.

MEGAN. Oh, I was shot.
Right outside that door. Actually.
So, I can make a joke.

MIKE. Can you believe they put up all the pictures?

MEGAN. We can't pretend it didn't happen.

EDDIE. *(To* MIKE:*)* That's what I tell him.

MIKE. Don't.

MEGAN. Sore subject?

EDDIE. He won't talk about it. I'm surprised he came.

MEGAN. He saved my life.

DAVID. What?

EDDIE. What?

MEGAN. Yeah.

MIKE. No, I didn't.

MEGAN. You did.

MIKE. I did what anybody would have done.

MEGAN. Bull.

EDDIE. What happened?

MIKE. Let's change the—

MEGAN. We were running down the hallway and before I knew it, I was shot. Hit right above my pelvic bone.

MIKE. It could have been either of us.

MEGAN. But it wasn't.

(To EDDIE *and* DAVID:*)*

So I'm lying there and he keeps running. Mike almost made it to a classroom when I called out his name. He turned, saw me bleeding and ran back.

MIKE. Well you still owed me like six bucks.

MEGAN. Will you stop deflecting?

MIKE. It's not a big deal.
Just instinct.

MEGAN. I'm not going to let you minimize this. You could have been shot.

MIKE. Not even close.

MEGAN. James hadn't left the hallway yet.

(*Back to the story:*)

He sees I'm bleeding and tries to stop the flow of blood. But his hands weren't stemming it. So he ripped his shirt off like some bad eighties action hero and held it over my stomach to stop the blood flow. To top it off, he shielded me with his body.
He stayed like that until the paramedics came.
They said I would have died from blood loss if it wasn't for Mike.

(*A silence falls over the table.*
EDDIE *kisses* MIKE *on the temple and hugs him close.*)

DAVID. Thank you.

MEGAN. You know what I thought that whole time?

MIKE. What?

MEGAN. I have to get friggen shot for you to lay your shirtless body on top of me?!?
I should have known you were gay.

(*The table bursts into laughter.*
MEGAN *reaches her hand out and touches* MIKE's *arm.*)

MIKE. You should come visit us.
Meet the kids.
Teach them a little basketball.

MEGAN. I will. Because I know you're not teaching them anything about basketball.

MIKE. Trash talk?

MEGAN. Wanna go outside and settle this?

MIKE. The kids'll love you.

MEGAN. No deflecting.
Let's find a ball.

>*(Black.)*

Raleigh—Football Field

>*(The clash of men slamming their bodies into each other. Helmets crashing. A coach's whistle.*
>COACH *appears, played by* JAMES.*)*

COACH. Let's go ladies. Take five!

>*(*COACH *disappears.*
>There's RALEIGH, *all handsome in full football gear, helmet in one hand. Water in another. He drinks before he speaks.)*

RALEIGH. Football is my life.
Always has been. When I was a little baby, I slept with a football.
I remember my dad drilling it into me when I played Pop Warner how important it was that I go pro. He always told me that, at the very least, football would pay for my college education. But if I was good enough—
I could be drafted by the NFL.
Make millions, buy a house, marry a Playboy Bunny, and retire after only working seven years.
Never having to work again.
But only if I was good enough.
I didn't love school or have direction so it sounded pretty good to me.
I worked and I worked and I worked so hard to make my dad proud.
He pulled me out of the Pop Warner football league when I was eight because they didn't keep individual stats. Put me in a league that was three hours away. He'd have to pull me out of school early sometimes so I could make games and practices on time.
See, he wanted to track my stats against the other kids so he could monitor how well I was doing.
Use it to show people. Scouts.
Gain interest in me.
I started out as quarterback, but I blew out my shoulder when I was fourteen. I was fast as hell, so they made me a wide receiver, which—
don't tell my dad—
I liked a whole lot more.
Less pressure. I'm no good with pressure.
Last year, we won a state championship. I was a junior, rode the pine a lot, but damn!!!—
If that wasn't the best day of my life.

My dad was so proud.

Before that day, he never looked at me with such pride. Not even when I aced tests or got my driver's license.

He's done it once since.

Just this beaming pride.

He thinks I didn't start much because I wasn't a senior. But I know it was because I wasn't really good enough. When the scouts come to watch the team, they never paid me any attention.

Even the Division Two schools weren't showing any interest. And because my dad was always pulling me out of school I never really had good grades.

...

So, I guess it all works out.

I guess it was good that James shot me.

I was number six.

He got me in a classroom.

I was trying to hold the door closed. I braced it with my body. I mean, I don't know why I didn't think the bullets would go through the door, but they did.

I was shot seventeen times.

It was the last one that did it.

Hit my heart.

I went pretty quick, after the last one.

My body blocked him from opening the door.

Saved a bunch of freshmen.

Pathetic, huh?

Taking a computer class with a bunch of freshmen because I couldn't pass it the other two times I took it.

I mean, it's good.

I'd hate to think I'd be alive at fifty working some dead-end construction job with blown-out knees to match my blown-out shoulder, knowing I peaked as a junior in high school.

I'd hate to see the disappointment on my dad's face when I didn't make it to the NFL.

This way the peak works out, happened at the right time.

This way I get a full page in the yearbook.

This way I'm always remembered like this.

My prime.

This way I don't have to avoid all those embarrassing questions at the high school reunions.

This way football can always be my life.

...

...

Oh, the other time my dad looked at me with pride?

When he looked in my casket.

The freshmen all came to the funeral and told him what I did.
…
…
That—
That was nice of them.

> *(The coach's whistle blows again. RALEIGH starts to put on his helmet, but something stops him. Just for a moment. Is he going to say something else? Then, the helmet goes on and he joins his team.*
> *Another whistle. The crash of bodies.*
> *Black.)*

Molly—A Bookstore

> *(A small round of applause and a couple of boos as MOLLY enters and sits at a table with a stack of books next to her. The cover of the book is a picture of her and James.)*

MOLLY. I've cancelled the rest of the tour, can we please just keep this civil.

> *(A male HECKLER, played by JAMES, shouts out:)*

HECKLER. He killed my brother.

> *(She looks disappointed. Weary.)*

MOLLY. I know.
I was there.

HECKLER. And you're making money from it.

MOLLY. Please don't make me kick you out. Please.

HECKLER. How dare you defend that bastard.

> *(She nods her head and a BULKY MAN enters. He approaches the HECKLER.)*

BULKY MAN. Out.

HECKLER. She's a bitch out to scam us.

BULKY MAN. Time to go.

> *(The HECKLER shouts as the BULKY MAN drags him out.)*

HECKLER. Don't read her book. You're what's wrong with America. What if it was your brother? Trying to get rich on the backs of dead kids. You're disgusting and belong in hell with your boyfriend.

> *(The HECKLER is gone.)*

(Tears form in MOLLY's *eyes.)*

MOLLY. I'm sorry.
I don't like that.
I don't like to have that happen, but it's gotten pretty hairy up here.
The big lug is for everybody's protection.

(She picks up her book.)

The book's called *Understanding James.*
And it's a retrospective of all my thoughts on James from first meeting, until now.
The book is made up of various parts. Some diary entries from before the shooting. Some after. Some chapters are my thoughts after reading studies and research and consulting with therapists.
Talking with James's family.
Talking with James's best friend and the current expert in spree shootings: Dr. Sean Northman.
That kind of thing.
About two years ago I went back and reread my diaries from that time and this entry I'm about to read to you in particular is what prompted me to write the book.
It describes the first independent thought I had about the shooting.
And I realized it was the first time someone tried to understand James and not just crucify him.
It's what I wanted to tell people when I heard them talking about James and the shooting.
The section was written about two months after the shooting.

(She opens the book but stops herself.)

Oh, I should mention that those diary entries are virtually untouched thoughts from the mind of a child. I cleaned up spelling and whatnot, but that's it.

(She opens the book, but slowly closes it.)

You know…I lied.
I've been lying this whole press tour.
That untouched thing is just something I tell people.
It is my diary from that time. And everything is factual.
But I lied when I said it's only cleaned up a little.
I did some big time editing.
I don't know why I say that.
Perhaps to protect me from my detractors. Distance and—
Honestly, I don't know why I told you the truth now. But there it is.
Anyway.

(She reads.)

We kinda dated once.

Not like seriously or anything. Just one date.

And we went to a dance together.

And we hung out at his place a couple of times.

This was all last year. Way before he killed all those kids.

And he broke it off with me so I didn't have anything to do with the shooting. It's not like I jilted him and that's the reason—

I don't have a ton of friends. Neither does he.

A lot of people thought he was strange—

A lot of people think I'm strange—

They just didn't know him. He could be a really sweet guy.

One time his dad was supposed to pick him up from school—

See, James's mom and dad got a divorce and James's dad never really came around. He was more interested in a bottle, if you know what I mean.

And, to tell you the truth, I think he might of been in jail or something. It's just an impression I got from the kinds of things said at James's house.

Besides the point, he never got to see his dad and his dad was supposed to pick him up one day and hang out with him. James thought his dad was awesome.

Hated his mom. Thought she was the reason the family broke up.

But I guess most kids hate the parent they live with and idolize the one that's not around.

So, his dad doesn't show. Instead of getting angry or something, he came and picked me up and took me for cheese fries. Said it's what his dad used to do with him.

He wanted to cry, but he didn't.

I felt bad for him.

James was really smart. He said, "You can't choose your real family, but you can always choose those you make family."

And he told me he wanted to make me family.

And that's when he started crying.

He told me he loved me.

Said he would never do anything to hurt me like his family hurt him.

…

…

He broke up with me like a week later.

Said he wasn't really that interested anymore because I wouldn't put out.

At first I thought it might be true—

…

Then I realized, I think he's just afraid of his emotions. Showing them, I mean.

It's vulnerable.

My mom always said he didn't know love. But I think he knew it. I mean, I showed him plenty of love.

I think he just didn't understand what to do with it.

…

…

On the day of the shooting, we all heard the shots in the classrooms. People were scared. I thought I was going to die. This girl, Janelle, came running down the hall and into my classroom. She was freaking out, had some blood on her. She wasn't saying a lot that made sense, but I heard her say James did it.

I was out of the classroom before the teacher could stop me.

My class was at the end of a hallway. I walked past eight classrooms full of people.

I could hear panicked screams, cries of pain.

The gunshots were getting closer.

When I got to the end of the hallway—

I saw James.

I yelled his name and he turned to me. I said "what are you doing?"

He told me to move.

He wanted to go down the hallway.

Again, I asked "what are you doing?"

He pointed the gun at me and told me to move. Said he had things to do.

I told him he'd have to shoot me to get by. He shoved me and made a move to get around me, but I stepped in front of him.

He told me he'd fucking kill me.

Sorry, but that's what he said.

"Remember the cheese fries? What about the family we choose? Are you going to break that promise you made to me? Again?"

He looked like he was going to cry.

I moved towards him and he stepped back real fast.

He put his gun to his head.

And boom.

…

…

They said I saved a lot of people.

And I'm proud of that.

I just—

I have to wonder—

…

I hate that people keep talking about what an awful person he is.

Or try to simplify what he did.

What his life came to is not an easy answer. He was a complicated kid and there were a lot of factors.

People forget that.
...
He was still my friend.
He'll always be my first boyfriend.
The first person I loved.
The first boy I kissed.
And there's nothing wrong with me so how could there be something wrong with him?
I wish people would remember he is still someone's son.
He's still human.
He's still the first person I chose to be my family.
...
I try not to say that often because it doesn't get me any friends.
And when I told my mom, she slapped me.
But I think it does need to be said.

> (MOLLY *closes the book.*)

Questions?

> (*Black.*)

Janelle—Narcotics Anonymous Meeting

> (*A small round of applause. Maybe eight people.*
> *We find ourselves in a small room at Lincoln High School. About eight people sit in a circle [the group is played by the* SHOOTERS.]
> *Most hold a coffee or water bottle.*
> *Some look put together. Some look terrible.*
> *One of the put-together ones speaks. He is the* GROUP LEADER.)

GROUP LEADER. Anybody else want to speak tonight?

> (*His eyes fall on a particularly messed-up-looking girl. This is* JANELLE.)

GROUP LEADER. Janelle.

> (*She shakes her head no. Her* SPONSOR, *played by* JAMES, *reaches out and touches her shoulder.*)

SPONSOR. You can do this.

JANELLE. I can't.

SPONSOR. You came back here, didn't you?
You're clean, aren't you?
You're Wonder Woman.
You can do anything.

(She smiles at him.)

SPONSOR. Who are you?

JANELLE. I'm Wonder Woman.

SPONSOR. Goddamn right you are!

(She nods.
Stands.)

JANELLE. Hi, my name is Janelle.

(The group responds:)

GROUP. Hi, Janelle.

JANELLE. I'm addicted to...
Anything that will make me forget.
Mostly heroin...when I could afford it.

(The group laughs. She smiles.
It feels good.)

JANELLE. I've been completely clean three weeks.
And other than two setbacks, I've been clean almost nine months.
I lost a lot of progress, but I'll get it back.
This isn't my normal meeting. But I wanted to use real bad tonight.
So I called my sponsor and he found a meeting.
Ironic the only meeting is here at Lincoln High School. I didn't want to come.
But that should show you how hard I'm trying to kick this.
This is the place I'm trying to forget.
This school has ghosts.
...
...

SPONSOR. Face your ghosts.

(She smiles.)

JANELLE. I was a student here at Lincoln when—
...
I don't usually talk about this.
When James Smith killed all those people.
I didn't have an off-school lunch pass, but I ditched with my friends, KC and Marcelle.
They were eating ice cream.
Vanilla.
Soft serve.
We were just sneaking back onto campus. We were running late.
I needed gas.

I thought we'd have enough to get back. But we ran out.

The gas station was only a block away from where the car stopped, so we pushed the car there.

Three girls.

I remember I thought we were strong.

Badasses.

Invincible.

Able to do anything the boys could do. But with more style and substance.

I bought them ice cream at the gas station for helping me push. It's what friends do.

KC had a billion tardies already. Another one and she'd be suspended. So we had to be super careful when we came back in.

Marcelle kept talking about prom. A senior had asked her out.

It's silly—

She was so concerned. She was afraid she'd have to put out or something. I remember I told her it wasn't 1982 anymore and those forever ago "rules" were dumb and outdated and she didn't have to put out if she didn't want to and if she was expected to because it was prom or whatever, then the boy she was with wasn't worthy of her, her time, or her "flower."

That was the biggest concern we had.

And we actually called it her flower.

What idiots.

…

That's when the shots came.

I could tell they were close.

Before we could run, he came around the corner. He looked at me.

James.

Everyone always thought he was a freak.

Me too, honestly.

But I didn't think he'd do something like that. Everyone thought he was such a freak, they usually went out of their way to be mean to him.

He looked at me.

And then KC.

And Marcelle.

Marcelle dropped her ice cream and screamed.

He shot her first.

In the face.

He had to sweep the gun across my path to get from one to the other.

And then he shot KC in the chest.

Then he smiled at me.

It was kind.

I had seen it before. A week earlier, he forgot a pen and I let him have one. When he tried to give it back at the end of first period, I told him to keep it for the rest of the day. He asked if I didn't want it back because he had touched it.

That made me sad for him.

I told him no, that's silly. He would need it for the rest of the day and he can give me the pen back in the morning. That's when he smiled the kind smile. He told me he owed me one.

I didn't think of that in the moment when he killed Marcelle and KC. I only thought of that after.

I wonder if they gave him a pen—

…

When I shoot up, I forget.

Just go to another world.

It's like a switch that turns my brain off.

I forget that if I hadn't run out of gas we'd have been in class in a hallway that he never went near and my friends would still be alive.

…

If he really wanted to pay back my kindness he would have shot me when he shot them.

Maybe that's what I was trying to do when I shot up. Too scared for suicide so maybe go for an accidental on purpose overdose.

Be able to forget forever.

…

I watched James walk around the corner. Towards this very classroom, actually.

The image I can't get of my head, the one that keeps me doped up? It's not my two friends.

Or even him.

It's the melting vanilla ice cream and the blood. The two puddles overlapped.

Pure white and dark red mixing in the middle to make the prettiest shade of pink I've ever seen.

…

…

It might have been a mistake coming here.

I want to use so bad.

> *(She cries. Hard. Harder than anybody else.*
> *Hers are the first tears we see in the play.*
> *Her SPONSOR stands up and holds her.)*

SPONSOR. You don't have to use.

> *(The group leader joins the hug. So do all the others.)*

GROUP LEADER. We got you covered.

(JANELLE *bawls from the middle of the group.*)

JANELLE. Thank you. Thank you. Thank you.

(*Black.*)

Sean—A University

(*A simple podium.*
A MODERATOR, *played by* JAMES, *approaches.*)

MODERATOR. Ladies and gentleman, I'm so excited. Dr. Sean Northman is a brilliant mind who has been studying spree shootings and the psychology of spree shooters ever since he was involved in the incident at Lincoln High School. Folks, Dr. Sean Northman.

(*The* MODERATOR *steps back and* SEAN *approaches the podium.*)

SEAN. Thank you.
This isn't my normal lecture—
I've been inspired.
I hope you've all read Molly's book, *Understanding James.* It's been inspiring to me in that she talks about her experience.
I've never really talked about my experience before.
I've always remained a bit—
…
Removed.

(SEAN *looks to the podium and organizes his notes. His eyes look up and he's in speech mode. The affable man from before has been transformed into something serious. It makes him look older.*)

SEAN. My best friend killed fourteen people.
That puts his spree at Lincoln High School number five on the list of most deadly school shootings behind Virginia Tech, Sandy Hook, University of Texas, and Columbine.
Thirty-three.
Twenty-seven.
Sixteen.
Fifteen.
And fourteen.
…
I've done a ton of research to try and—
Understand, or—
…
You know, I think, everybody wants the answers, but nobody is asking the right questions.
I don't know.

Honestly, I still struggle to make—
Seung-Hui Cho got his thirty-three kills in thirty-six minutes of shooting.
It only took Adam Lanza ten minutes to kill twenty-eight.
Mostly kindergartners.
Charles Whitman sat in a clock tower and picked off sixteen people over ninety-six minutes on a lazy August afternoon at the University of Texas.
Eric Harris and Dylan Klebold tag-teamed to kill fifteen people in fifty-one minutes.
Which brings us to James.
James killed fourteen people I knew in seventeen minutes.
That's one hundred and five dead kids and teachers in less than three hours and thirty minutes of elapsed time.
I tell you, all this research. I've tried...
But I can't make real sense of any of it.
It's messed up.
But I know facts. Statistics.
A lot of people find meaning in facts.
...
In 2013 there were thirty-three incidents of gun violence on school property in the U.S. That's almost three a month.
What's really screwed up? In the thirty days after Adam Lanza killed twenty-seven five-year-olds, there were nine school shootings.
While an entire country was in mourning, nine people thought it was a good idea to enter a school with a gun and cause havoc.
...
I don't know what any of this means. And most of these shooters wind up dead so we can't ask questions.
I mean, something is happening. There is an escalation. There has to be a reason.
People are so quick to blame video games or violent movies or TV shows. They blame gun control laws: we should have it, we shouldn't.
They blame automatic weapons. They blame bullying or teachers or parents.
They call the shooters loners or losers.
Say they have mental deficiencies.
They blame depression, retardation, mental health, medications.
And I'm sure all of those things can and do factor, in one way or another, but any single one of those is just an oversimplification of the greater problem.
It's ignoring the complexities and holding those shooters at an arm's distance.
Like we could have "fixed" them if we solved that one simple problem.

If only they didn't play *Grand Theft Auto*.
Or watch *Kill Bill*.
Or took an anti-depressant.
Or didn't take an anti-depressant.
Or had more friends.
Or didn't have access to guns.
It gives us this false idea that we can somehow stop it from happening again. And it gives parents and friends and the community as a whole something to hate and point a finger at.
It gives the media buzzwords and a great story.
A villain.
But in these situations, nobody is bad. Or born evil.
James wasn't.
To be clear, I'm not condoning his actions. He had a major, major lapse in judgment. But he wasn't evil.
…
You've all heard the term "suicide cluster"?
It's a documented phenomenon.
For example, one kid in a small town commits suicide, several others follow shortly after. The kids don't have to know each other…they can even be from different high schools and have different reasons for the suicide. But either way, there is a spike in suicides when compared to the national average.
Studies show that hearing about a suicide seems to make those who are vulnerable feel they have permission to do it, especially if they feel close to or know somebody who was close to or feel they are in the same circumstances as the original suicide. It can spread by word of mouth, but—
…
also
by
the
media.
…
The month Marilyn Monroe died, there were over two hundred more suicides than the national average.
Upon learning of someone else's suicide, people can decide that the action of suicide is appropriate for them as well, especially if the publicized suicide was of someone in a similar situation as them.
People imitate those who seem similar, despite or even because of societal disapproval.
Because of this, many countries, such as Norway and Turkey, do not mention or publicize suicide in the media.
Another interesting fact about suicide: many people interviewed after the suicide of a relative or friend have a tendency to simplify

the issues; their grief can lead to their minimizing or ignoring significant factors.

...

I know. I thought this was about school shootings, not suicides. What is this guy talking about?

Well—

...

In the month following the twenty-four-hour news media coverage of Adam Lanza killing twenty-eight people in Newtown, there were nine school shootings. Adam Lanza's rampage falls on the heels of James Holmes killing twelve and injuring seventy in a theater in Colorado just a few short miles from the first highly publicized school shooting in Columbine.

I don't know, but maybe our obsession with idolizing these shooters or reducing them down to people who play video games or who have been bullied is sending a pretty scary message to those kids who do play video games or who are being bullied that this is an answer.

That shooting up a school is an answer.

But then again, that's just oversimplifying.

And even though I've studied this for years, I don't claim to have the answers.

I just have the facts.

The statistics.

That's thirty-three, twenty-seven, sixteen, fifteen, and fourteen dead.

All including the shooter.

Let's not forget they were victims too.

They are people.

Not simply villains.

I'm not suggesting we sympathize.

I'm asking that we empathize.

Try to find the truth.

The truth of those shooters in us.

Not look for the simple excuse.

But

the

truth.

...

And the truth is my best friend in high school killed fourteen of our classmates.

And he wasn't a terrible guy.

He just did a terrible thing.

And nobody will ever know why.

...

...

(He takes a moment. He opens his mouth as if he wants to say something else, but decides against it.)

SEAN. Thank you.

(A stunned silence falls over the crowd.
Black.)

James—A Void—Blackness—Outside of Time and Space

(It's never quite clear if the light finds JAMES, or JAMES finds the light.
He delivers the monologue in the house, walking amongst the audience. Reaching out, taking hands, making eye contact, sitting next to people, walking through rows. He absolutely could be one of these people. One of these people could be him.)

JAMES. Hello…everybody.
I've never been able to speak clearly.
I get these ideas and then I vomit them out. But try to follow me. Please.
When I was a child and thought of my future, I always imagined I'd be a great lover of women. Rich. Famous maybe. I'd cure cancer or be a great writer. An actor. A football player.
I was always going to be good at sports.
When I closed my eyes, my future was bright. Always on the grandest scale. I thought I'd be the best. A researcher. Scientist. That my life would be the best.
I was special and destined for greatness.
I knew it.
One in a million.
But I guess every kid thinks that way.
Nobody says when I grow up I want to be divorced. Be a failure as a husband and a father.
As a kid, my dad didn't think that.
Or lose my job. Have a mental illness or end up in a wheelchair. Be bullied. Be a bully.
I want to be an alcoholic. Or an addict.
Nobody wants to beat their wife and nobody wants to murder. Or rape. Be a pedophile.
But these kinds of people are out there.
When you're little, the path from childhood to adulthood is easy. You can see it.
That's part of the illusion.
This is where adults fail children. Where teachers and parents suck.

Here.
When they fail to tell us that not everybody can win in the end.
That's for the few.
The other people.
They should sit us down and say "You see that over there? Take a good look. This is as close as you're getting."
It's not being mean, it's being realistic.
Not everybody's dream comes true. Sometimes you wander off the path and end up—
...
When you are young you always hear it's going to be better. Your life is full of potential. But old people always talk about the good old days and youth being wasted on the young. So, I guess, when is it ever good?
When are you anything really?
...
Or maybe you're just born defective.
That's the easy answer.
The one they always want to give when something like this happens.
But easy answers are bullshit.
You know, that's something else they should teach us kids— The adults, I mean.
They should teach us that life is solitude. It's not something you experience with others.
We are each marching forward in unison, separately.
And sometimes that solitude becomes so loud that you lose all track of yourself.
Values you hold close dissipate.
To be my age and know the path that was so clear eight years ago will never appear again—
That it's lost for you—

> (*He has found his way onto the stage. He stands in the darkness, only illuminated from the house lights bleeding onto the stage.*)

When that solitude becomes deafening, who knows how you'll react. Because when I was little, I certainly didn't wish my life would end up like this. That I would walk into a school and—
...
...
...
I'm sorry.
...
...
...
...

I'm really sorry.
…
…
…
…
…
I'm rambling.
This is part of my problem, I ramble.
I can't collect my thoughts.
People don't like it.

    (Blackout.)

ACT 3

(JAMES is lying on the ground in a prone position. He is out cold.
The room matches the void of JAMES's monologue.
In it are six men, all observing the body in front of them.
CHO is the true alpha.
WHITMAN and LANZA each think they are the alpha. They
defer to CHO, but not to each other.
HARRIS and KLEBOLD are the babies. Just a couple of kids.
KLEBOLD follows HARRIS's every move. They are often found
playing on a PS4.
The one named RODGER is apart from the group. He hides in the
corners and the shadows. He is covered in bruises, welts, and cuts.
His face is almost unrecognizable as a face.
They watch JAMES. After a long moment:)

CHO. Arrivals are happening with greater frequency.

RODGER. Our message is getting out.

LANZA. Shut up, Rodger.

WHITMAN. Someone get Spencer.

LANZA. You go, bitch.

KLEBOLD. What do you think his number is?

HARRIS. Why do you think he did it?

KLEBOLD. Yeah. Why do you think he did it?

CHO. Wake him.

WHITMAN. Spencer isn't—

CHO. Wake. Him.

> *(WHITMAN very kindly tries to shake JAMES awake. JAMES*
> *still sleeps.*
> *LANZA, finding this annoying, pushes WHITMAN away and*
> *slaps JAMES across the face.*
> *JAMES starts to stir but the others don't notice as WHITMAN*
> *and LANZA are engaged in a shoving battle.)*

WHITMAN. Put your hands on me again I'll beat you till you look
like Rodger.

> *(The man named RODGER shrinks back at the sound of his name.)*

LANZA. One on one, I'll kill you.
Jarhead.

WHITMAN. I'm not a six-year-old, Lanza. So that might be tough
for you.

LANZA. Oh-rah. Bitch.

CHO. Stop it.

> (HARRIS *and* KLEBOLD *enter the fray to keep the men separated.*)

LANZA. I looked them in the face. Not from a—

CHO. Stop it!!

> (*The men stop.*)

CHO. He's waking.

> (WHITMAN *gets down to* JAMES's *level and offers a helping hand.*)

WHITMAN. Welcome, James.

LANZA. Shut up, boy scout.

JAMES. Who are you?

CHO. Ask him why he did it.

LANZA. Why'd you do it?

WHITMAN. Give the kid a chance—

LANZA. Shut up, Whitman.

WHITMAN. Think you're so tough?

LANZA. Got a higher count than you.

WHITMAN. I'm surprised you can count. Need to take your shoes off to make it to twenty?

LANZA. Yeah. And I still need eight more digits to count my kills.

HARRIS. You just sat in a tower picking people off.

KLEBOLD. You weren't in the thick of it.

WHITMAN. There were two of you morons, so technically your number should be halved.

HARRIS. Again?

KLEBOLD. Standby argument.

LANZA. (*Mock whining:*) Little baby so sad that his number didn't hold up. Wha wha wha.

WHITMAN. I'd love to gut you Lanza.
Killing babies?
Real tough.

KLEBOLD. I hate to agree with jarhead.

HARRIS. Yo, Klebold. Lanza's bomb at *Call of Duty.*

KLEBOLD. Truth.
So right, Harris.

>*(LANZA pretends to shoot a rifle around the room. Aims the last shot at WHITMAN.)*

LANZA. Pop. Pop. Pop.

JAMES. I love *Call of Duty!*

>*(The room goes quiet.*
>*A long moment.)*

CHO. Why did you do it?
She'll want to know.

>*(The room remains silent as they all watch JAMES.)*

LANZA. Speak up or we'll toss you in the corner with Rodger.

WHITMAN. You're lucky we let you out of that corner, Lanza.

>*(LANZA loses it.)*

LANZA. Shut up!

CHO. Children.

>*(They stop.)*

CHO. Why did you do it?

>*(JAMES shrugs his shoulders.)*

JAMES. I guess—
…
I guess I was mad and I wanted people to pay.

>*(CHO smiles. The others laugh.)*

CHO. What were you mad about?

>*(JAMES shrugs his shoulders again.)*

CHO. Easier question?

JAMES. Yes, please.

WHITMAN. Boy's got manners. Take notes, Lanza.

>*(LANZA shoots him a look but CHO's hand is up and silencing him before LANZA can speak.)*

CHO. What did you use?

JAMES. Four Glocks and a shotgun.

LANZA. Kills?

(Tension fills the air. A lot rides on this answer.)

JAMES. Fourteen.

(A celebration.)

LANZA. Yes!! Still second.

WHITMAN. Injured?

LANZA. Injuries count for shit.

WHITMAN. It's 'cause you're dead last with two.
Injuries?

JAMES. Um—
Nineteen.
I think.

WHITMAN. That puts you fourth if we count by incidents.
Three if you count by individual totals.

HARRIS. Give it a rest.

KLEBOLD. It's like a broken record.

HARRIS. Tired of hearing it.

KLEBOLD. Yeah, tired of hearing it.

CHO. Shut up.

(The room goes silent. CHO makes a decision.)

CHO. Introduce yourselves.

LANZA. Adam Lanza.
Sandy Hook.
Twenty-eight dead.
Two injured.

WHITMAN. Charles Whitman.
University of Texas, Austin.
Sixteen dead.
Thirty-two injured.

HARRIS. Eric Harris.

KLEBOLD. Dylan Klebold.

KLEBOLD and HARRIS. Columbine.

KLEBOLD. Columbine.

HARRIS. Fifteen killed.

KLEBOLD. Twenty-one injured.

CHO. Seung-Hui Cho.
Virginia Tech.
Thirty-three dead.
Twenty-three injured.

JAMES. Hi.
I'm James Smith.
Fourteen killed.
Nineteen injured.
But you knew that.

CHO. Rodger.

(*A long moment. RODGER doesn't respond.*)

CHO. Did we cut his tongue out?

WHITMAN. No.

LANZA. Can we?

CHO. Maybe.
Speak, Rodger.

(*No answer.*)

CHO. I believe I said speak, Rodger.

(*Small moment before he talks. It's painful for him to talk.*)

RODGER. Elliot Rodger.
University of California, Santa Barbara.
Seven dead.
Thirteen injured.

(*WHITMAN kicks him.*)

LANZA. Shouldn't even be here with us.

WHITMAN. Gives us a bad name.

(*Finally, something WHITMAN and LANZA can agree on.*)

(*A female appears out of the shadows. When she speaks, everyone snaps to attention. There is a real reverence. She is like a mother/ goddess/lover figure. She is ethereal. Her touch can be both sexual or maternal, depending on the moment.*)

SPENCER. Brenda Spencer.
I killed two and injured nine picking people off at Cleveland Elementary School from the comfort of my own home with the gun my daddy bought me for Christmas.
…

(*She steps toward JAMES, uncomfortably close.*)

SPENCER. Please don't try to screw me.

JAMES. I wouldn't.

SPENCER. Why?

> *(She moves closer. This flusters him.)*

SPENCER. Is there something wrong with me?

JAMES. No.
I just—
I was—
Only being—
I won't try to do that with you.

SPENCER. Good.

> *(She points to* RODGER.*)*

'Cause he did.

> *(The boys start laughing.)*

JAMES. What?

LANZA. Nobody touches Mama without paying the price.

WHITMAN. Unless she wants to be touched.

> *(Was that a look shared between* WHITMAN *and* SPENCER?*)*

LANZA. I swear to god Whitman—

CHO. She's the reason we're all here.

WHITMAN. Well, not me.

> *(They all look at him.)*

WHITMAN. Are we going to ignore history? I pre-date her by thirteen years.

HARRIS. She's a legend.

KLEBOLD. Yeah. A legend.

CHO. The first modern shooter.
The rest of us born of her.

> *(She gives* WHITMAN *a moment of special attention. Her touch with him is sexual. He likes it. The other boys get jealous.)*

SPENCER. Charles, *you* inspire *me*.
But I take the onus on me like you never could. It's why I'm responsible for all who came after.
…
Except for Rodger. He's a pig.

(They all find this funny. JAMES laughs to fit in.)

LANZA. Mama, tell the new kid what you told the reporter when he asked you why you did it?

(SPENCER likes the idea and pats LANZA like a child.)

SPENCER. I told the man "I don't like Mondays."

LANZA. Can you believe that?
So elegant and amazing.

JAMES. That can't be the reason she did it.
Is it?

(She shrugs her shoulders.)

LANZA. Don't question Mama.

SPENCER. It's a fair question, Adam.

(Her hand on him and he melts. Backs down.)

SPENCER. Truth?
I did want to get on TV.
And everyone made fun of me 'cause I was ugly.
And a lesbian.
My dad was an alcoholic.
I was suicidal.
Lived in poverty.

(She lovingly reaches out and caresses JAMES's face and hair as she speaks.)

SPENCER. I asked my dad for a radio for Christmas and he bought me a gun. I think he wanted me to kill myself.
He beat me.
And raped me.
And I was drinking.
And on drugs.
And I have an injured temporal lobe.

(JAMES's face is in her hands.)

SPENCER. And I seriously hate Mondays.

*(Long pause.
She moves away from JAMES.)*

JAMES. All that true?

WHITMAN. As far as we know.

CHO. Yes. It is.

JAMES. What about the rest of you? Why'd you do it?

(They all just sort of shrug.)

SPENCER. Gentlemen, answer the boy's question.
Seung-Hui, you first.

CHO. Violent movies, I guess.
Kill Bill. RoboCop. Cannibal Holocaust. Rambo. The *Saw* flicks.
Battle Royale.
And porn.
Rape porn.

HARRIS. We were video games.

KLEBOLD. YEAH!
DOOM!!

HARRIS. We were freaking obsessed!

KLEBOLD. Never stopped playing!
I was once up for thirty-six straight hours playing that game!!

HARRIS. I made a mod!
My life's work!!
Made a level look just like the school.

KLEBOLD. Practiced killing there. So rad!
Oh! And *Mortal Kombat*!!

HARRIS. *GoldenEye 007*!!!

KLEBOLD. *Grand Theft Auto*!!!!

HARRIS. Three! Four!! *Vice City*!!! All the *GTAs*!!!!

CHO. You know they said I played *Counter-Strike*.

HARRIS. AHHHHHHH!!! Love that game!!!!!
I didn't know you played Cho!!!!!
You Windows or Xbox?!?!?

CHO. I never played.
I hate video games.

KLEBOLD. Dude.
Not.
Cool.

LANZA. You know, at first, they gave credit for my work to my brother Ryan. Pissed me off.
He's a huge *Mass Effect* fan.
He's never hurt a fly. Weakness.
Media spread a story that I was obsessed with *Call of Duty*.
Never even tried the game until these two idiots pulled me into it.
…

I am kind of obsessed now.

JAMES. So why'd you do it?

LANZA. Don't you know?
I had access to guns and I'm a freaking loony.
That simple. Or so it seems.
…
My dad, after I killed the twenty-eight, he told the media he wished
I was aborted.
Said he always wanted to abort me.
Get rid of me.
He meant like before the shooting.
Like before I was born.

SPENCER. Adam.
He didn't mean it.
He was lashing out.

LANZA. Thanks, Mama.
But I think he meant it.
It's why I'm all messed up.

> *(A moment. Nobody knows what to say.*
> WHITMAN, *unexpectedly, comes to* LANZA's *rescue.)*

WHITMAN. Marines.
I saw stuff. War games. They taught me violence.
Just a cycle of violence.
It was in me.

> *(A long beat.)*

SPENCER. I don't like Mondays.

> *(They all laugh.)*

JAMES. *(Referring to* RODGER:*)* How about him?

> *(The mood in the room sours.)*

LANZA. No one gives a crap.

> *(There is a long pause.)*

SPENCER. Speak, Rodger.

> *(Another moment.)*

RODGER. I had a problem with—

SPENCER. Truthful.

RODGER. I hate women.

LANZA. Tell him what you said. Virgin.

RODGER. I'm a 22-year-old—

WHITMAN. On your feet!

(RODGER, *with great difficulty, stands up.*)

RODGER. I'm a 22—

WHITMAN. Loud and proud. Like the video.

RODGER. I'm a 22-year-old virgin. I didn't understand why women wouldn't sleep with me. I'm the perfect guy. A supreme gentleman and all they wanted was obnoxious guys. So I wanted to kill all the sluts in the sororities who repeatedly denied my sexual advances. If I couldn't have the girls, I was going to destroy them. They denied me my happiness. I deserved my happiness. I deserved what they were giving away. I deserved—

(WHITMAN *cuts him off with a hard right hook to the face.*)

WHITMAN. You don't deserve anything. Women, like Mama, have rights.

SPENCER. Our bodies are not your privilege.

RODGER. We all took lives!

LANZA. Still, you're the biggest cockroach.

RODGER. Don't act like you're better than me. Like you hate me for what I did. You hate me 'cause I'm the new guy.

LANZA. Maybe.

RODGER. Lanza killed kindergartners.

WHITMAN. And he took his turn.

RODGER. Bunch of cowards. Pack mentality. Need to feel superior.

WHITMAN. Someone needs to be bottom of the food chain.

LANZA. You'll do for now.

RODGER. You're worse than those obnoxious frat boys. Attacking one of your own.

LANZA. You are not one of us!!

HARRIS. You thought you were rotting in loneliness before?

KLEBOLD. Who's the alpha male now, bitch?

(CHO *steps forward between the boys. They part like the Red Sea. They think he's going to say something, but instead he dislodges a giant loogie from his throat and spits it on* RODGER. *He pulls his hand back to punch* RODGER.)

SPENCER. Enough.

> *(The circle stops closing in around* RODGER. *After a moment, it disperses.*
> *A long pause.)*

JAMES. I don't want to be the new guy.

SPENCER. You won't be for long.

CHO. And we like you.

JAMES. Really?!

CHO. Sure.

JAMES. Awesome! I knew I was like you guys.

SPENCER. We can be your family, James. If you choose us.

JAMES. Okay. Yeah!

> *(A moment.)*

How old are you guys?

CHO. Whitman is the oldest at 25.
I'm 23.

> *(Referring to* RODGER:*)*

Dipshit is 22.

> *(Points to* LANZA:*)*

20.
Harris is 18.
Klebold is 17.

> *(Points to* SPENCER:*)*

And Mama is 16.

WHITMAN. The youngest.

LANZA. The best.

> *(*JAMES *thinks of something.)*

JAMES. Umm—

CHO. What?

JAMES. Where are we?

> *(Nobody says anything for a long time.)*

CHO. We're immortal.

JAMES. Wait.

No.
I'm dead.
I put the gun to my own head and pulled the trigger.

LANZA. We all did.

WHITMAN. Not me.

> *(They all look at him.)*

WHITMAN. What?
I was shot by the cops.

LANZA. You're splitting hairs and you know it.
Okay, jerk.
You were suicide by cop. But still a suicide.

JAMES. But... We're all dead.

HARRIS. Mama isn't.

JAMES. What?

WHITMAN. She's sitting in a jail cell somewhere.

CHO. Yet, we live free.
Anytime someone brings a gun to school.

HARRIS. Or a violent video game comes out.

KLEBOLD. Or movie.

WHITMAN. Or doesn't take a woman's no for an answer.

LANZA. Or identifies someone as the loner kid.

SPENCER. Or when a parent drops their kid off for school in the morning.
...
...
...
...
They think of us.
Not the real us, but this version of us.
This collective consciousness.
In the minds of the people we touched—
Affected—
We are the boogeymen.
Youth and immortality.
That's what we have.
They don't have that. They are always getting older.

(ROBERT, MEGAN, MIKE, RALEIGH, JANELLE, MOLLY, SARA, *and* SEAN *appear on the fringes of the stage surrounding the* SHOOTERS.)

JAMES. If, say, someone reached out to you—
…
Would you have done it?
…
…
Would any of you do it again?

WHITMAN. Any takers?

LANZA. Kind of a loaded question.

(HARRIS *and* KLEBOLD *shake their heads as if to say "don't look at us."*)

CHO. I guess we'll never know.

JAMES. Fair enough.
I have one more question.

CHO. Shoot.

JAMES. Is it better?
Do any of you feel any better after the shooting?

(*The* SHOOTERS *don't respond. Their silence speaks volumes.*)

JAMES. Okay.

SPENCER. What about you?

JAMES. What about me?

(*The entire cast [except for* JAMES*] speaks in unison.*)

ALL. (*Except* JAMES:) Do you feel better?

(JAMES *takes a long moment to think. He opens his mouth to speak: Blackout.*)

End of Play